BUDGET
IT!

Created & Designed By
TeeCee Design Studio

BOOK TITLE: _______________________________

EDITING:

FORMATTING:

COVER:

PROMOTIONAL GRAPHICS:

BLOG TOURS:

SWAG:

GIFTS:

PRINT COPIES:

AD/PROMOTIONS:

OTHER COSTS:

TOTAL COSTS:

BOOK TITLE: _______________________________

EDITING:

FORMATTING:

COVER:

PROMOTIONAL GRAPHICS:

BLOG TOURS:

SWAG:

GIFTS:

PRINT COPIES:

AD/PROMOTIONS:

OTHER COSTS:

TOTAL COSTS:

BOOK TITLE: _______________________________

EDITING:

FORMATTING:

COVER:

PROMOTIONAL GRAPHICS:

BLOG TOURS:

SWAG:

GIFTS:

PRINT COPIES:

AD/PROMOTIONS:

OTHER COSTS:

TOTAL COSTS:

BOOK TITLE: _______________________________

EDITING:

FORMATTING:

COVER:

PROMOTIONAL GRAPHICS:

BLOG TOURS:

SWAG:

GIFTS:

PRINT COPIES:

AD/PROMOTIONS:

OTHER COSTS:

TOTAL COSTS:

BOOK TITLE: _______________________________

EDITING:

FORMATTING:

COVER:

PROMOTIONAL GRAPHICS:

BLOG TOURS:

SWAG:

GIFTS:

PRINT COPIES:

AD/PROMOTIONS:

OTHER COSTS:

TOTAL COSTS:

BOOK TITLE: _______________________________________

EDITING:

FORMATTING:

COVER:

PROMOTIONAL GRAPHICS:

BLOG TOURS:

SWAG:

GIFTS:

PRINT COPIES:

AD/PROMOTIONS:

OTHER COSTS:

TOTAL COSTS:

BOOK TITLE: _______________________________________

EDITING:

FORMATTING:

COVER:

PROMOTIONAL GRAPHICS:

BLOG TOURS:

SWAG:

GIFTS:

PRINT COPIES:

AD/PROMOTIONS:

OTHER COSTS:

____

____

____

____

____

____

____

____

____

____

TOTAL COSTS:

BOOK TITLE: ________________________________

EDITING:

FORMATTING:

COVER:

PROMOTIONAL GRAPHICS:

BLOG TOURS:

SWAG:

GIFTS:

PRINT COPIES:

AD/PROMOTIONS:

OTHER COSTS:

TOTAL COSTS:

BOOK TITLE: _______________________________

EDITING:

FORMATTING:

COVER:

PROMOTIONAL GRAPHICS:

BLOG TOURS:

SWAG:

GIFTS:

PRINT COPIES:

AD/PROMOTIONS:

OTHER COSTS:

____

____

____

____

____

TOTAL COSTS:

BOOK TITLE: ____

EDITING:

FORMATTING:

COVER:

PROMOTIONAL GRAPHICS:

BLOG TOURS:

SWAG:

GIFTS:

PRINT COPIES:

AD/PROMOTIONS:

OTHER COSTS:

TOTAL COSTS:

BOOK TITLE: ___________________________

EDITING:

FORMATTING:

COVER:

PROMOTIONAL GRAPHICS:

BLOG TOURS:

SWAG:

GIFTS:

PRINT COPIES:

AD/PROMOTIONS:

OTHER COSTS:

TOTAL COSTS:

BOOK TITLE: _______________________________________

EDITING:

FORMATTING:

COVER:

PROMOTIONAL GRAPHICS:

BLOG TOURS:

SWAG:

GIFTS:

PRINT COPIES:

AD/PROMOTIONS:

OTHER COSTS:

TOTAL COSTS:

BOOK TITLE: ___________________________________

EDITING:

FORMATTING:

COVER:

PROMOTIONAL GRAPHICS:

BLOG TOURS:

SWAG:

GIFTS:

PRINT COPIES:

AD/PROMOTIONS:

OTHER COSTS:

TOTAL COSTS:

BOOK TITLE: _______________________________

EDITING:

FORMATTING:

COVER:

PROMOTIONAL GRAPHICS:

BLOG TOURS:

SWAG:

GIFTS:

PRINT COPIES:

AD/PROMOTIONS:

OTHER COSTS:

TOTAL COSTS:

BOOK TITLE: _______________________________

EDITING:

FORMATTING:

COVER:

PROMOTIONAL GRAPHICS:

BLOG TOURS:

SWAG:

GIFTS:

PRINT COPIES:

AD/PROMOTIONS:

OTHER COSTS:

TOTAL COSTS:

BOOK TITLE: _______________________________________

EDITING:

FORMATTING:

COVER:

PROMOTIONAL GRAPHICS:

BLOG TOURS:

SWAG:

GIFTS:

PRINT COPIES:

AD/PROMOTIONS:

OTHER COSTS:

TOTAL COSTS:

BOOK TITLE: _______________________________

EDITING:

FORMATTING:

COVER:

PROMOTIONAL GRAPHICS:

BLOG TOURS:

SWAG:

GIFTS:

PRINT COPIES:

AD/PROMOTIONS:

OTHER COSTS:

TOTAL COSTS:

BOOK TITLE: _______________________________________

EDITING:

FORMATTING:

COVER:

PROMOTIONAL GRAPHICS:

BLOG TOURS:

SWAG:

GIFTS:

PRINT COPIES:

AD/PROMOTIONS:

OTHER COSTS:

TOTAL COSTS:

BOOK TITLE: ___________________________________

EDITING:

FORMATTING:

COVER:

PROMOTIONAL GRAPHICS:

BLOG TOURS:

SWAG:

GIFTS:

PRINT COPIES:

AD/PROMOTIONS:

OTHER COSTS:

TOTAL COSTS:

BOOK TITLE: _______________________________

EDITING:

FORMATTING:

COVER:

PROMOTIONAL GRAPHICS:

BLOG TOURS:

SWAG:

GIFTS:

PRINT COPIES:

AD/PROMOTIONS:

OTHER COSTS:

TOTAL COSTS:

BOOK TITLE: ____________________________

EDITING:

FORMATTING:

COVER:

PROMOTIONAL GRAPHICS:

BLOG TOURS:

SWAG:

GIFTS:

PRINT COPIES:

AD/PROMOTIONS:

OTHER COSTS:

TOTAL COSTS:

BOOK TITLE: _______________________________

EDITING:

FORMATTING:

COVER:

PROMOTIONAL GRAPHICS:

BLOG TOURS:

SWAG:

GIFTS:

PRINT COPIES:

AD/PROMOTIONS:

OTHER COSTS:

____

____

____

____

____

____

____

____

____

____

TOTAL COSTS:

BOOK TITLE: _______________________________

EDITING:

FORMATTING:

COVER:

PROMOTIONAL GRAPHICS:

BLOG TOURS:

SWAG:

GIFTS:

PRINT COPIES:

AD/PROMOTIONS:

OTHER COSTS:

TOTAL COSTS:

BOOK TITLE: _____________________________________

EDITING:

FORMATTING:

COVER:

PROMOTIONAL GRAPHICS:

BLOG TOURS:

SWAG:

GIFTS:

PRINT COPIES:

AD/PROMOTIONS:

OTHER COSTS:

TOTAL COSTS:

BOOK TITLE: ______________________________

EDITING:

FORMATTING:

COVER:

PROMOTIONAL GRAPHICS:

BLOG TOURS:

SWAG:

GIFTS:

PRINT COPIES:

AD/PROMOTIONS:

OTHER COSTS:

TOTAL COSTS:

BOOK TITLE: _______________________________

EDITING:

FORMATTING:

COVER:

PROMOTIONAL GRAPHICS:

BLOG TOURS:

SWAG:

GIFTS:

PRINT COPIES:

AD/PROMOTIONS:

OTHER COSTS:

TOTAL COSTS:

BOOK TITLE: _______________________

EDITING:

FORMATTING:

COVER:

PROMOTIONAL GRAPHICS:

BLOG TOURS:

SWAG:

GIFTS:

PRINT COPIES:

AD/PROMOTIONS:

OTHER COSTS:

TOTAL COSTS:

BOOK TITLE: _______________________________________

EDITING:

FORMATTING:

COVER:

PROMOTIONAL GRAPHICS:

BLOG TOURS:

SWAG:

GIFTS:

PRINT COPIES:

AD/PROMOTIONS:

OTHER COSTS:

____

____

____

____

____

TOTAL COSTS:

BOOK TITLE: ______________________________________

EDITING:

FORMATTING:

COVER:

PROMOTIONAL GRAPHICS:

BLOG TOURS:

SWAG:

GIFTS:

PRINT COPIES:

AD/PROMOTIONS:

OTHER COSTS:

____

____

____

____

____

TOTAL COSTS:

BOOK TITLE: ___________________________________

EDITING: [ ]

FORMATTING: [ ]

COVER: [ ]

PROMOTIONAL GRAPHICS: [ ]

BLOG TOURS: [ ]

SWAG: [ ]

GIFTS: [ ]

PRINT COPIES: [ ]

AD/PROMOTIONS: [ ]

OTHER COSTS:

______________ [ ]   ______________ [ ]

______________ [ ]   ______________ [ ]

______________ [ ]   ______________ [ ]

______________ [ ]   ______________ [ ]

______________ [ ]   ______________ [ ]

TOTAL COSTS: [ ]

BOOK TITLE: ___________________________________

EDITING:

FORMATTING:

COVER:

PROMOTIONAL GRAPHICS:

BLOG TOURS:

SWAG:

GIFTS:

PRINT COPIES:

AD/PROMOTIONS:

OTHER COSTS:

TOTAL COSTS:

BOOK TITLE: _______________________________

EDITING:

FORMATTING:

COVER:

PROMOTIONAL GRAPHICS:

BLOG TOURS:

SWAG:

GIFTS:

PRINT COPIES:

AD/PROMOTIONS:

OTHER COSTS:

TOTAL COSTS:

BOOK TITLE: _________________________________

EDITING:

FORMATTING:

COVER:

PROMOTIONAL GRAPHICS:

BLOG TOURS:

SWAG:

GIFTS:

PRINT COPIES:

AD/PROMOTIONS:

OTHER COSTS:

TOTAL COSTS:

BOOK TITLE: ___________________________________

EDITING:

FORMATTING:

COVER:

PROMOTIONAL GRAPHICS:

BLOG TOURS:

SWAG:

GIFTS:

PRINT COPIES:

AD/PROMOTIONS:

OTHER COSTS:

TOTAL COSTS:

BOOK TITLE: ___________________________

EDITING:

FORMATTING:

COVER:

PROMOTIONAL GRAPHICS:

BLOG TOURS:

SWAG:

GIFTS:

PRINT COPIES:

AD/PROMOTIONS:

OTHER COSTS:

TOTAL COSTS:

BOOK TITLE: ___________________________________

EDITING:

FORMATTING:

COVER:

PROMOTIONAL GRAPHICS:

BLOG TOURS:

SWAG:

GIFTS:

PRINT COPIES:

AD/PROMOTIONS:

OTHER COSTS:

TOTAL COSTS:

BOOK TITLE: _______________________________

EDITING:

FORMATTING:

COVER:

PROMOTIONAL GRAPHICS:

BLOG TOURS:

SWAG:

GIFTS:

PRINT COPIES:

AD/PROMOTIONS:

OTHER COSTS:

TOTAL COSTS:

BOOK TITLE: ________________________________

EDITING:

FORMATTING:

COVER:

PROMOTIONAL GRAPHICS:

BLOG TOURS:

SWAG:

GIFTS:

PRINT COPIES:

AD/PROMOTIONS:

OTHER COSTS:

TOTAL COSTS:

BOOK TITLE: _______________________________

EDITING:

FORMATTING:

COVER:

PROMOTIONAL GRAPHICS:

BLOG TOURS:

SWAG:

GIFTS:

PRINT COPIES:

AD/PROMOTIONS:

OTHER COSTS:

TOTAL COSTS:

BOOK TITLE: ______________________________

EDITING:

FORMATTING:

COVER:

PROMOTIONAL GRAPHICS:

BLOG TOURS:

SWAG:

GIFTS:

PRINT COPIES:

AD/PROMOTIONS:

OTHER COSTS:

TOTAL COSTS:

BOOK TITLE: _______________________________

EDITING:

FORMATTING:

COVER:

PROMOTIONAL GRAPHICS:

BLOG TOURS:

SWAG:

GIFTS:

PRINT COPIES:

AD/PROMOTIONS:

OTHER COSTS:

TOTAL COSTS:

BOOK TITLE: _______________________________

EDITING:

FORMATTING:

COVER:

PROMOTIONAL GRAPHICS:

BLOG TOURS:

SWAG:

GIFTS:

PRINT COPIES:

AD/PROMOTIONS:

OTHER COSTS:

TOTAL COSTS:

BOOK TITLE: ___________________________________

EDITING:

FORMATTING:

COVER:

PROMOTIONAL GRAPHICS:

BLOG TOURS:

SWAG:

GIFTS:

PRINT COPIES:

AD/PROMOTIONS:

OTHER COSTS:

TOTAL COSTS:

BOOK TITLE: ___________________________________

EDITING:

FORMATTING:

COVER:

PROMOTIONAL GRAPHICS:

BLOG TOURS:

SWAG:

GIFTS:

PRINT COPIES:

AD/PROMOTIONS:

OTHER COSTS:

TOTAL COSTS:

BOOK TITLE: _______________________________

EDITING:

FORMATTING:

COVER:

PROMOTIONAL GRAPHICS:

BLOG TOURS:

SWAG:

GIFTS:

PRINT COPIES:

AD/PROMOTIONS:

OTHER COSTS:

____

____

____

____

____

TOTAL COSTS:

BOOK TITLE: _______________________________

EDITING:

FORMATTING:

COVER:

PROMOTIONAL GRAPHICS:

BLOG TOURS:

SWAG:

GIFTS:

PRINT COPIES:

AD/PROMOTIONS:

OTHER COSTS:

TOTAL COSTS:

BOOK TITLE: __________________________________

EDITING:

FORMATTING:

COVER:

PROMOTIONAL GRAPHICS:

BLOG TOURS:

SWAG:

GIFTS:

PRINT COPIES:

AD/PROMOTIONS:

OTHER COSTS:

TOTAL COSTS:

BOOK TITLE: ______________________________

EDITING: [ ]

FORMATTING: [ ]

COVER: [ ]

PROMOTIONAL GRAPHICS: [ ]

BLOG TOURS: [ ]

SWAG: [ ]

GIFTS: [ ]

PRINT COPIES: [ ]

AD/PROMOTIONS: [ ]

OTHER COSTS:

______________ [ ]   ______________ [ ]

______________ [ ]   ______________ [ ]

______________ [ ]   ______________ [ ]

______________ [ ]   ______________ [ ]

______________ [ ]   ______________ [ ]

TOTAL COSTS: [ ]

BOOK TITLE: ___________________________________

EDITING:

FORMATTING:

COVER:

PROMOTIONAL GRAPHICS:

BLOG TOURS:

SWAG:

GIFTS:

PRINT COPIES:

AD/PROMOTIONS:

OTHER COSTS:

TOTAL COSTS:

BOOK TITLE: ___________________________________

EDITING: [ ]

FORMATTING: [ ]

COVER: [ ]

PROMOTIONAL GRAPHICS: [ ]

BLOG TOURS: [ ]

SWAG: [ ]

GIFTS: [ ]

PRINT COPIES: [ ]

AD/PROMOTIONS: [ ]

OTHER COSTS:

____________	[ ]	____________	[ ]
____________	[ ]	____________	[ ]
____________	[ ]	____________	[ ]
____________	[ ]	____________	[ ]
____________	[ ]	____________	[ ]

TOTAL COSTS: [ ]

BOOK TITLE: ___________________________________

EDITING:

FORMATTING:

COVER:

PROMOTIONAL GRAPHICS:

BLOG TOURS:

SWAG:

GIFTS:

PRINT COPIES:

AD/PROMOTIONS:

OTHER COSTS:

TOTAL COSTS:

BOOK TITLE: _______________________________

EDITING:

FORMATTING:

COVER:

PROMOTIONAL GRAPHICS:

BLOG TOURS:

SWAG:

GIFTS:

PRINT COPIES:

AD/PROMOTIONS:

OTHER COSTS:

TOTAL COSTS:

BOOK TITLE: _______________________________

EDITING:

FORMATTING:

COVER:

PROMOTIONAL GRAPHICS:

BLOG TOURS:

SWAG:

GIFTS:

PRINT COPIES:

AD/PROMOTIONS:

OTHER COSTS:

TOTAL COSTS:

BOOK TITLE: _______________________________

EDITING:

FORMATTING:

COVER:

PROMOTIONAL GRAPHICS:

BLOG TOURS:

SWAG:

GIFTS:

PRINT COPIES:

AD/PROMOTIONS:

OTHER COSTS:

TOTAL COSTS:

BOOK TITLE: ____

EDITING:

FORMATTING:

COVER:

PROMOTIONAL GRAPHICS:

BLOG TOURS:

SWAG:

GIFTS:

PRINT COPIES:

AD/PROMOTIONS:

OTHER COSTS:

TOTAL COSTS:

BOOK TITLE: ______________________________

EDITING:

FORMATTING:

COVER:

PROMOTIONAL GRAPHICS:

BLOG TOURS:

SWAG:

GIFTS:

PRINT COPIES:

AD/PROMOTIONS:

OTHER COSTS:

TOTAL COSTS:

BOOK TITLE: _______________________________

EDITING:

FORMATTING:

COVER:

PROMOTIONAL GRAPHICS:

BLOG TOURS:

SWAG:

GIFTS:

PRINT COPIES:

AD/PROMOTIONS:

OTHER COSTS:

TOTAL COSTS:

BOOK TITLE: _______________________________________

EDITING: [ ]

FORMATTING: [ ]

COVER: [ ]

PROMOTIONAL GRAPHICS: [ ]

BLOG TOURS: [ ]

SWAG: [ ]

GIFTS: [ ]

PRINT COPIES: [ ]

AD/PROMOTIONS: [ ]

OTHER COSTS:

______________ [ ]   ______________ [ ]

______________ [ ]   ______________ [ ]

______________ [ ]   ______________ [ ]

______________ [ ]   ______________ [ ]

______________ [ ]   ______________ [ ]

TOTAL COSTS: [ ]

BOOK TITLE: ______________________________

EDITING:

FORMATTING:

COVER:

PROMOTIONAL GRAPHICS:

BLOG TOURS:

SWAG:

GIFTS:

PRINT COPIES:

AD/PROMOTIONS:

OTHER COSTS:

TOTAL COSTS:

BOOK TITLE: _______________________________

EDITING:

FORMATTING:

COVER:

PROMOTIONAL GRAPHICS:

BLOG TOURS:

SWAG:

GIFTS:

PRINT COPIES:

AD/PROMOTIONS:

OTHER COSTS:

TOTAL COSTS:

BOOK TITLE: ______________________________________

EDITING:

FORMATTING:

COVER:

PROMOTIONAL GRAPHICS:

BLOG TOURS:

SWAG:

GIFTS:

PRINT COPIES:

AD/PROMOTIONS:

OTHER COSTS:

TOTAL COSTS:

BOOK TITLE: _______________________________

EDITING:

FORMATTING:

COVER:

PROMOTIONAL GRAPHICS:

BLOG TOURS:

SWAG:

GIFTS:

PRINT COPIES:

AD/PROMOTIONS:

OTHER COSTS:

TOTAL COSTS:

BOOK TITLE: _______________________________

EDITING:

FORMATTING:

COVER:

PROMOTIONAL GRAPHICS:

BLOG TOURS:

SWAG:

GIFTS:

PRINT COPIES:

AD/PROMOTIONS:

OTHER COSTS:

TOTAL COSTS:

BOOK TITLE: ______________________________________

EDITING:

FORMATTING:

COVER:

PROMOTIONAL GRAPHICS:

BLOG TOURS:

SWAG:

GIFTS:

PRINT COPIES:

AD/PROMOTIONS:

OTHER COSTS:

TOTAL COSTS:

BOOK TITLE: _______________________________

EDITING:

FORMATTING:

COVER:

PROMOTIONAL GRAPHICS:

BLOG TOURS:

SWAG:

GIFTS:

PRINT COPIES:

AD/PROMOTIONS:

OTHER COSTS:

_______________   _______________

_______________   _______________

_______________   _______________

_______________   _______________

_______________   _______________

TOTAL COSTS:

BOOK TITLE: _______________________________

EDITING:

FORMATTING:

COVER:

PROMOTIONAL GRAPHICS:

BLOG TOURS:

SWAG:

GIFTS:

PRINT COPIES:

AD/PROMOTIONS:

OTHER COSTS:

TOTAL COSTS:

BOOK TITLE: _______________________________

EDITING:

FORMATTING:

COVER:

PROMOTIONAL GRAPHICS:

BLOG TOURS:

SWAG:

GIFTS:

PRINT COPIES:

AD/PROMOTIONS:

OTHER COSTS:

TOTAL COSTS:

BOOK TITLE: _______________________________

EDITING:

FORMATTING:

COVER:

PROMOTIONAL GRAPHICS:

BLOG TOURS:

SWAG:

GIFTS:

PRINT COPIES:

AD/PROMOTIONS:

OTHER COSTS:

TOTAL COSTS:

BOOK TITLE: _______________________________________

EDITING:

FORMATTING:

COVER:

PROMOTIONAL GRAPHICS:

BLOG TOURS:

SWAG:

GIFTS:

PRINT COPIES:

AD/PROMOTIONS:

OTHER COSTS:

____

____

____

____

____

____

____

____

____

____

TOTAL COSTS:

BOOK TITLE:

EDITING:
FORMATTING:
COVER:
PROMOTIONAL GRAPHICS:
BLOG TOURS:
SWAG:
GIFTS:
PRINT COPIES:
AD/PROMOTIONS:

OTHER COSTS:

TOTAL COSTS:

BOOK TITLE: ________________________________

EDITING:

FORMATTING:

COVER:

PROMOTIONAL GRAPHICS:

BLOG TOURS:

SWAG:

GIFTS:

PRINT COPIES:

AD/PROMOTIONS:

OTHER COSTS:

TOTAL COSTS:

BOOK TITLE: _______________________________

EDITING:

FORMATTING:

COVER:

PROMOTIONAL GRAPHICS:

BLOG TOURS:

SWAG:

GIFTS:

PRINT COPIES:

AD/PROMOTIONS:

OTHER COSTS:

TOTAL COSTS:

BOOK TITLE: _______________________________

EDITING:

FORMATTING:

COVER:

PROMOTIONAL GRAPHICS:

BLOG TOURS:

SWAG:

GIFTS:

PRINT COPIES:

AD/PROMOTIONS:

OTHER COSTS:

TOTAL COSTS:

BOOK TITLE: _______________________________

EDITING:

FORMATTING:

COVER:

PROMOTIONAL GRAPHICS:

BLOG TOURS:

SWAG:

GIFTS:

PRINT COPIES:

AD/PROMOTIONS:

OTHER COSTS:

TOTAL COSTS:

BOOK TITLE: ___________________________________

EDITING:

FORMATTING:

COVER:

PROMOTIONAL GRAPHICS:

BLOG TOURS:

SWAG:

GIFTS:

PRINT COPIES:

AD/PROMOTIONS:

OTHER COSTS:

TOTAL COSTS:

BOOK TITLE: _______________________________

EDITING:

FORMATTING:

COVER:

PROMOTIONAL GRAPHICS:

BLOG TOURS:

SWAG:

GIFTS:

PRINT COPIES:

AD/PROMOTIONS:

OTHER COSTS:

TOTAL COSTS:

BOOK TITLE: _______________________________

EDITING:

FORMATTING:

COVER:

PROMOTIONAL GRAPHICS:

BLOG TOURS:

SWAG:

GIFTS:

PRINT COPIES:

AD/PROMOTIONS:

OTHER COSTS:

TOTAL COSTS:

BOOK TITLE: _______________________________

EDITING:

FORMATTING:

COVER:

PROMOTIONAL GRAPHICS:

BLOG TOURS:

SWAG:

GIFTS:

PRINT COPIES:

AD/PROMOTIONS:

OTHER COSTS:

TOTAL COSTS:

BOOK TITLE: _______________________________

EDITING:

FORMATTING:

COVER:

PROMOTIONAL GRAPHICS:

BLOG TOURS:

SWAG:

GIFTS:

PRINT COPIES:

AD/PROMOTIONS:

OTHER COSTS:

TOTAL COSTS:

BOOK TITLE: _______________________________

EDITING:

FORMATTING:

COVER:

PROMOTIONAL GRAPHICS:

BLOG TOURS:

SWAG:

GIFTS:

PRINT COPIES:

AD/PROMOTIONS:

OTHER COSTS:

TOTAL COSTS:

BOOK TITLE: _______________________________

EDITING:

FORMATTING:

COVER:

PROMOTIONAL GRAPHICS:

BLOG TOURS:

SWAG:

GIFTS:

PRINT COPIES:

AD/PROMOTIONS:

OTHER COSTS:

TOTAL COSTS:

BOOK TITLE: _______________________________

EDITING: [ ]

FORMATTING: [ ]

COVER: [ ]

PROMOTIONAL GRAPHICS: [ ]

BLOG TOURS: [ ]

SWAG: [ ]

GIFTS: [ ]

PRINT COPIES: [ ]

AD/PROMOTIONS: [ ]

OTHER COSTS:

_______________	[ ]	_______________	[ ]
_______________	[ ]	_______________	[ ]
_______________	[ ]	_______________	[ ]
_______________	[ ]	_______________	[ ]
_______________	[ ]	_______________	[ ]

TOTAL COSTS: [ ]

BOOK TITLE: _______________________________

EDITING:

FORMATTING:

COVER:

PROMOTIONAL GRAPHICS:

BLOG TOURS:

SWAG:

GIFTS:

PRINT COPIES:

AD/PROMOTIONS:

OTHER COSTS:

TOTAL COSTS:

BOOK TITLE: ______________________________

EDITING:

FORMATTING:

COVER:

PROMOTIONAL GRAPHICS:

BLOG TOURS:

SWAG:

GIFTS:

PRINT COPIES:

AD/PROMOTIONS:

OTHER COSTS:

TOTAL COSTS:

BOOK TITLE: ___________________________________

EDITING:

FORMATTING:

COVER:

PROMOTIONAL GRAPHICS:

BLOG TOURS:

SWAG:

GIFTS:

PRINT COPIES:

AD/PROMOTIONS:

OTHER COSTS:

___________________   ___________________

___________________   ___________________

___________________   ___________________

___________________   ___________________

___________________   ___________________

TOTAL COSTS:

BOOK TITLE: ______________________________

EDITING:

FORMATTING:

COVER:

PROMOTIONAL GRAPHICS:

BLOG TOURS:

SWAG:

GIFTS:

PRINT COPIES:

AD/PROMOTIONS:

OTHER COSTS:

______________ ______________

______________ ______________

______________ ______________

______________ ______________

______________ ______________

TOTAL COSTS:

BOOK TITLE: _______________________________

EDITING:

FORMATTING:

COVER:

PROMOTIONAL GRAPHICS:

BLOG TOURS:

SWAG:

GIFTS:

PRINT COPIES:

AD/PROMOTIONS:

OTHER COSTS:

TOTAL COSTS:

BOOK TITLE: ___________________________________

EDITING: | |

FORMATTING: | |

COVER: | |

PROMOTIONAL GRAPHICS: | |

BLOG TOURS: | |

SWAG: | |

GIFTS: | |

PRINT COPIES: | |

AD/PROMOTIONS: | |

OTHER COSTS:

TOTAL COSTS: | |

BOOK TITLE: _______________________________

EDITING:

FORMATTING:

COVER:

PROMOTIONAL GRAPHICS:

BLOG TOURS:

SWAG:

GIFTS:

PRINT COPIES:

AD/PROMOTIONS:

OTHER COSTS:

TOTAL COSTS:

BOOK TITLE: ____

EDITING:

FORMATTING:

COVER:

PROMOTIONAL GRAPHICS:

BLOG TOURS:

SWAG:

GIFTS:

PRINT COPIES:

AD/PROMOTIONS:

OTHER COSTS:

TOTAL COSTS:

BOOK TITLE: ______________________________

EDITING: [ ]

FORMATTING: [ ]

COVER: [ ]

PROMOTIONAL GRAPHICS: [ ]

BLOG TOURS: [ ]

SWAG: [ ]

GIFTS: [ ]

PRINT COPIES: [ ]

AD/PROMOTIONS: [ ]

OTHER COSTS:

______________ [ ]   ______________ [ ]

______________ [ ]   ______________ [ ]

______________ [ ]   ______________ [ ]

______________ [ ]   ______________ [ ]

______________ [ ]   ______________ [ ]

TOTAL COSTS: [ ]

BOOK TITLE: ______________________________

EDITING:

FORMATTING:

COVER:

PROMOTIONAL GRAPHICS:

BLOG TOURS:

SWAG:

GIFTS:

PRINT COPIES:

AD/PROMOTIONS:

OTHER COSTS:

TOTAL COSTS:

BOOK TITLE: ______________________________

EDITING:

FORMATTING:

COVER:

PROMOTIONAL GRAPHICS:

BLOG TOURS:

SWAG:

GIFTS:

PRINT COPIES:

AD/PROMOTIONS:

OTHER COSTS:

____

____

____

____

____

TOTAL COSTS:

BOOK TITLE: _______________________________________

EDITING:

FORMATTING:

COVER:

PROMOTIONAL GRAPHICS:

BLOG TOURS:

SWAG:

GIFTS:

PRINT COPIES:

AD/PROMOTIONS:

OTHER COSTS:

TOTAL COSTS:

BOOK TITLE: _______________________________

EDITING:

FORMATTING:

COVER:

PROMOTIONAL GRAPHICS:

BLOG TOURS:

SWAG:

GIFTS:

PRINT COPIES:

AD/PROMOTIONS:

OTHER COSTS:

TOTAL COSTS:

BOOK TITLE: ___________________________

EDITING:

FORMATTING:

COVER:

PROMOTIONAL GRAPHICS:

BLOG TOURS:

SWAG:

GIFTS:

PRINT COPIES:

AD/PROMOTIONS:

OTHER COSTS:

TOTAL COSTS:

BOOK TITLE: ___________________________________

EDITING:

FORMATTING:

COVER:

PROMOTIONAL GRAPHICS:

BLOG TOURS:

SWAG:

GIFTS:

PRINT COPIES:

AD/PROMOTIONS:

OTHER COSTS:

TOTAL COSTS:

BOOK TITLE: _______________________________

EDITING:

FORMATTING:

COVER:

PROMOTIONAL GRAPHICS:

BLOG TOURS:

SWAG:

GIFTS:

PRINT COPIES:

AD/PROMOTIONS:

OTHER COSTS:

TOTAL COSTS:

BOOK TITLE: _______________________________

EDITING:

FORMATTING:

COVER:

PROMOTIONAL GRAPHICS:

BLOG TOURS:

SWAG:

GIFTS:

PRINT COPIES:

AD/PROMOTIONS:

OTHER COSTS:

TOTAL COSTS:

BOOK TITLE: _______________________________

EDITING:

FORMATTING:

COVER:

PROMOTIONAL GRAPHICS:

BLOG TOURS:

SWAG:

GIFTS:

PRINT COPIES:

AD/PROMOTIONS:

OTHER COSTS:

TOTAL COSTS:

Thank you so much for your purchase.

I really do hope that this book has helped you,
even in some small way.

Would you like to see different designs/styles?

I am always very happy to hear from customers,
so please feel free to email me on

teeceedesignstudio@yahoo.com

www.ingramcontent.com/pod-product-compliance
Lightning Source LLC
Chambersburg PA
CBHW081309250726
48662CB00008B/2482